ISAAC ASIMOV'S
Library of the Universe

MARS:
Our Mysterious Neighbor

by Isaac Asimov

Gareth Stevens Publishing
Milwaukee

A special thanks to Gina Nelson (Jet Propulsion Laboratory) and Jody Swann (United States Geological Survey).

Library of Congress Cataloging-in-Publication Data

Asimov, Isaac, 1920-
   Mars: our mysterious neighbor.

   (Isaac Asimov's library of the universe)
   Bibliography: p.
   Includes index.
   Summary: Describes the characteristics of the fourth planet from the sun,
the only one whose surface can be seen in any detail from the earth.
   1. Mars (Planet)—Juvenile literature. [1. Mars (Planet) 2. Planets] I. Title.
II. Series: Asimov, Isaac, 1920-   Library of the universe.
QB641.A84   1988   523.4'3   87-42599
ISBN 1-55532-379-0
ISBN 1-55532-354-5 (lib. bdg.)

A Gareth Stevens Children's Books edition. Edited, designed, and produced by

Gareth Stevens, Inc.
7317 West Green Tree Road   Milwaukee, Wisconsin 53223, USA

Cover painting © Doug McLeod

Designer: Laurie Shock
Picture research: Kathy Keller
Artwork commissioning: Kathy Keller and Laurie Shock
Project editors: Mark Sachner and MaryLee Knowlton

Technical adviser and consulting editor: Greg Walz-Chojnacki

2 3 4 5 6 7 8 9 9 93 92 91 90 89 88

CONTENTS

Introduction

We live in the Universe, an enormously large place. It's only in the last 50 years or so that we've found out how large it really is.

It's only natural that we would want to understand the place we live in and in the last 50 years we have developed new instruments with which to get such understanding. We have radio telescopes, satellites, probes, and many other things that have told us far more about the Universe than could possibly be imagined when I was young.

Nowadays, we have seen planets up close. We have learned about quasars and pulsars, about black holes and supernovas. We have learned amazing facts about how the Universe may have come into being and how it may end. Nothing can be more astonishing and more interesting.

But not everything we see in the sky is brand-new. Thousands of years ago, people watched the sky and noticed that certain bright stars shifted position from night to night. The Greeks called them "wandering stars." Naturally, they called them that in the Greek language. Those words have come down to us to mean "planet."

One of these planets has a reddish color, almost the color of blood. It was therefore named after the god of war, Mars, since so much blood is spilled in war. In this book, I shall tell you about the planet Mars and what we have learned about it recently.

Mars, the planet most like Earth. People have long wondered if there could be life on Mars.

The Mystery of Mars

Let's leave Earth, heading away from the Sun. Mars is the first planet we come to. What do we know about our neighbor Mars? We know quite a bit, but Mars is a mysterious planet, too. We know that it is smaller than Earth. It is only half as wide as Earth, and it has only one-tenth Earth's mass. Still, Mars turns, or rotates, once every 24 1/2 hours. Its axis is tipped so that it has seasons like Earth's. Mars is colder, though, because it is farther from the Sun. It has ice caps at the poles. Of all the planets in our Solar system, it is most like Earth, so people naturally wondered if there were living creatures on Mars. If so, what were they like? That was the big mystery.

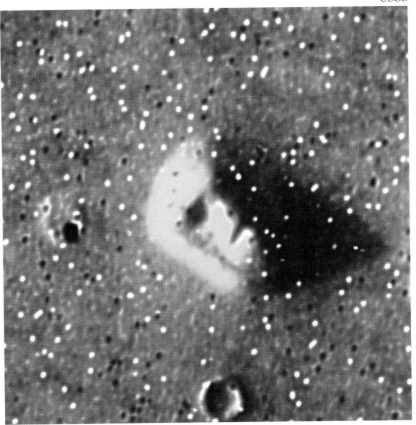

A remarkable photo of a detail on the surface of
Mars. Doesn't the object in the center look like a face?

Sunrise on Mars: a color-enhanced shot of the Martian landscape,
with a striking view of the Viking lander in the foreground.

A Desert World

We know that living creatures would have a hard time on Mars. Early astronomers could tell that it had only a thin atmosphere and that it must have very little water on it. Its surface might be one large desert. In 1877, however, narrow, dark markings were seen on Mars. These were studied by an American astronomer, Percival Lowell. He thought they were canals, dug by intelligent Martians to bring water from the ice caps at the poles to the desert areas in the rest of Mars. Lowell wrote several books on the subject, and for a while many people were sure there was intelligent life on Mars.

Lowell Observatory

Percival Lowell in a 1905 photograph. Here, he looks at Venus by daylight through a telescope that has been in continuous use since 1897.

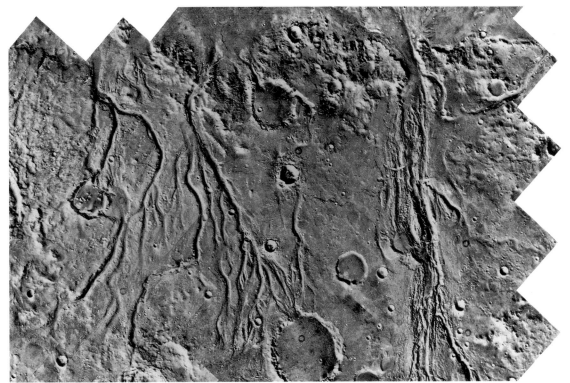

JPL

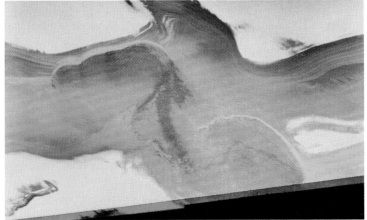

NASA

These channels on Mars' surface may have been carved by running water in Mars' distant past. These are not the same as the "canals" seen by Lowell. Astronomers now think the canals were an optical illusion.

Here is summer at Mars' North Pole. Clouds over the polar cap have cleared to reveal water ice, as well as the layered terrain beneath it.

Calling all Martians!

People were once so sure that Mars had intelligent beings on it that ways were thought up of sending them messages. One scientist suggested that huge triangles and squares be dug in Siberia, filled with oil, and set on fire at night. The Martians would see these through their telescopes, and then they might arrange something for us to see in return. Even as late as 1938, the actor Orson Welles presented a radio play in which Martians were said to be invading New Jersey. He frightened hundreds of people who got into their cars and drove away to escape those Martians — who really didn't exist.

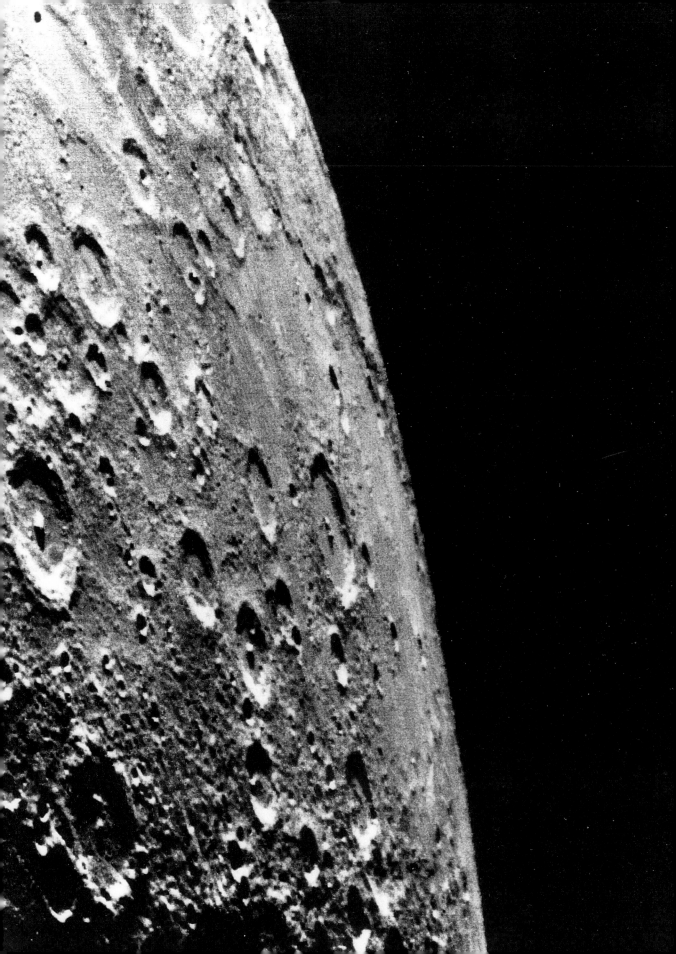

Moon-like Mars?

For years and years, people thought about the chances of life on Mars. Finally, when scientists learned how to send rockets to Mars, it seemed we would get some answers. In 1964, a Mars probe, Mariner 4, was sent out to Mars. In July, 1965, this probe passed within 6,000 miles (9,600 km) of the planet, and took 19 close-up photographs which it beamed back to Earth. These photographs showed craters on Mars like those on the Moon. Mars' atmosphere turned out to be only 1/100 as thick as Earth's, and there was no sign of any canals. Mars seemed to be a dead world.

NASA

The Mariner 4 television camera. The camera took pictures as it passed Mars, stored them on tape, and beamed them back to Earth. Each picture took about eight hours to play back, or reconstruct, from the radio transmission. The whole transmission lasted over seven days!

Left: The moon-like southern regions of Mars. After years of thinking about the possibility of life on Mars, scientists know it's not likely. Many people were relieved, but others were disappointed. How do you feel about it? Would you have liked to meet Martians?

JPL

Look Again!

In 1971, another Mars probe, Mariner 9, reached Mars. It went into orbit about Mars and took many photographs. It mapped almost the entire planet. There were definitely no canals. The photos showed that the straight, dark lines were just illusions. The photos also showed many craters on Mars, but also flatter areas with extinct volcanoes. One of these, named Olympus Mons, was far larger than any volcano on Earth. The pictures also showed a huge canyon, named Valles Marineris, that was far larger than our own Grand Canyon. Mars' surface proved to be much more interesting than that of the Moon. But it still seemed a dead world.

JPL

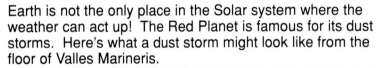

Earth is not the only place in the Solar system where the weather can act up! The Red Planet is famous for its dust storms. Here's what a dust storm might look like from the floor of Valles Marineris.

© John Foster 1988

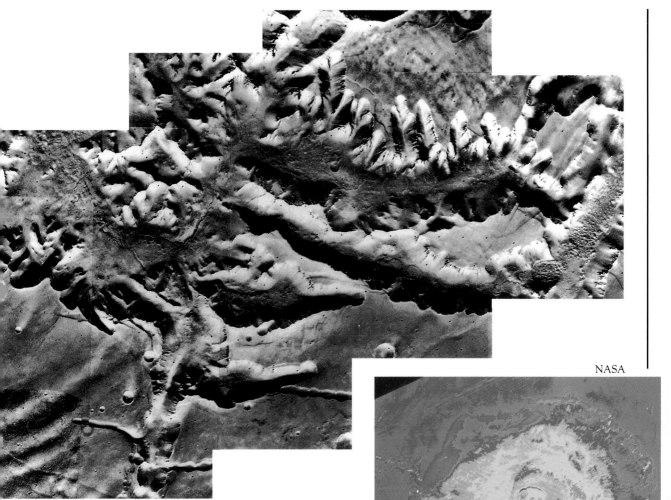

NASA

Ten Viking 1 pictures make up this image of a portion of western Valles Marineris. The channel-like formations were probably dug out by the wind and by the downhill flow of debris during ice thaws.

Olympus Mons, Mars' extinct volcano: This is the largest known volcano in the Solar system. This is a false-color photo taken by a Viking probe.

Mars — fooling the pros

Why did Percival Lowell see canals on Mars when there weren't any? He was a good astronomer with excellent telescopes. He worked on high ground in Arizona where the air was very clear. It's possible that he could just barely make out little dark patches on Mars. His eyes, not knowing what to make of them, saw them as straight lines. People have experimented with schoolchildren looking at distant circles with little dark patches. The children reported they saw straight lines. This is called an optical illusion. Maybe that's what fooled Lowell.

A New Look at Mars

In 1976, two new Mars probes arrived, Viking 1 and Viking 2. These were not there just to go into orbit about the planet. They were actually going to put landers on the Martian surface. They did this successfully. And while passing through the atmosphere, they analyzed it. The Martian atmosphere is about 95 percent carbon dioxide, and most of the rest is nitrogen and argon. This means that the Martian atmosphere has almost no oxygen in it. What's more the Martian surface is as cold as Antarctica or colder. So any water on Mars must be frozen.

More strange markings

The Mars probes have discovered strange markings on Mars. These markings look like dry river channels that form crookedly across the surface as real rivers would. Smaller channels run into larger ones just as smaller rivers run into larger ones on Earth. It seems almost certain that at one time in the past, Mars may have had liquid water forming rivers and, perhaps, lakes. In that case, what happened to the water? Is it now all frozen in the soil? And if Mars once had water and rivers, was the atmosphere thicker, then, and was there life on Mars, then? So far, we just don't know.

In 1976, Mars was photographed by Viking 1 from 348,000 miles (557,000 km) above the planet. Olympus Mons is visible near the upper left edge of the planet. Just to its right are the three volcanoes of the Tharsis ridge.

NASA

NASA

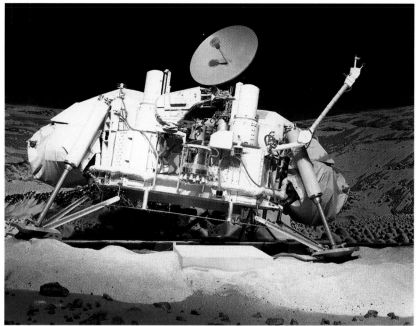

The Viking test lander: The front footpad of this model rests
on a rock, as the actual lander did on Mars. As a result,
cameras in the lander showed the Martian horizon to be
sloped. In fact, it is nearly perfectly level.

© John Waite 1987

At 86,592 feet (26,400 m), Olympus Mons is easily
taller than any of Earth's peaks. The back row shows
the Martian peaks. Center row, left to right, shows
Earth's Mt. Everest (29,028 ft / 8,850 m), Mt. Rainier
(14,410 ft / 4,393 m), and Mont Blanc (15,771 ft /
4,808 m). Front row shows Mt. Fuji (12,388 ft /
3,777 m) and Mt. St. Helens (9,677 ft / 2,950 m).

13

The Search for Life

The Viking probes took photographs of Mars' surface. But they also did more, for they carried equipment that could test the Martian soil. If the soil contained microscopic forms of life, the tests would show chemical changes. The probes scooped up soil and tested it in three different ways to see if such changes took place. There were changes, but it wasn't certain they were the result of life. However, nothing was detected in the soil that contained carbon, which is essential to our kind of life. Yes, the surface of Mars may be more interesting than that of our Moon. But it may still be that Mars is a dead world.

The surface of Mars looks like a rocky desert on Earth. The probes scooped up some of the Martian soil to test for life. None of our tests showed any signs of life.

NASA

The Martian horizon as photographed by the Viking lander. The lower
center of this beautiful shot shows trenches left by the lander's
sampling tools on the surface of Mars.

NASA

Another view of Mars from the lander. This is a colored shot of an area
similar to that shown in black and white on page 14.

The Moons of Mars

Mars has two small satellites, or moons, called Phobos and Deimos. They are not large globes like our own Moon, but they may be captured satellites that once passed Mars and were drawn into orbit by Mars' gravitational field. From Earth, they look like two dim dots of light, but the probes showed them more clearly. They are shaped like potatoes and are covered with craters. Phobos is 17 miles (27 km) across at its longest. Deimos is only 10 miles (16 km) across. Because of their small size and their closeness to Mars, these little satellites were not discovered till 1877. This was long after the more distant but larger satellites of Jupiter and Saturn were discovered.

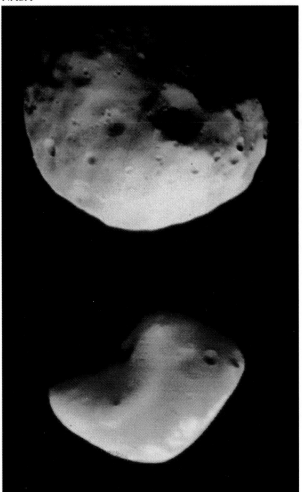

Martian satellites. Top: Phobos. Bottom: Deimos. Phobos orbits Mars in about seven hours and 40 minutes. Deimos orbits in about 30 hours.

If at first you don't succeed...

The Martian satellites were discovered by an American astronomer named Asaph Hall. Night after night in 1877, he looked through his telescope at the space near Mars and could find nothing. Finally, he made up his mind that it was no use. He said to his wife, whose maiden name was Angelina Stickney, that he was giving up. His wife said, "Try it one more night." He did, and discovered the satellites. Now the largest crater on the satellite Phobos is named "Stickney" in honor of the woman who urged Hall not to give up.

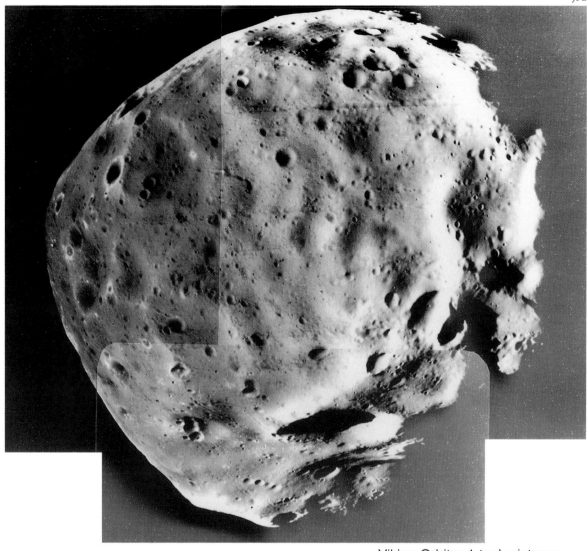

© Michael Carroll 1987

Viking Orbiter 1 took pictures that were combined to create this image of Phobos. The craters you see were probably caused by the impact of space debris.

The 1989 Soviet Phobos mission. One of its goals is to drop landers on Phobos to map its surface and subsurface and study its composition.

A Handful of Mars

Mars is much farther than the Moon and much harder to reach, but scientists are planning further probes. Both the Soviet Union and the US are planning to send probes to Mars and Phobos — including a possible joint USSR/US mission that will land and unload an automatic car like one used on the Moon. It could travel for miles across the Martian surface, studying the surface as it goes. Other probes might dig down and test the soil well beneath the surface. Even more exciting are probes that might collect samples of soil and then send them back to Earth. Such soil could be tested in great detail here on our own planet.

Phobos — a moon in a hurry!

*Phobos is only 5,810 miles (9,296 km) from Mars' center. Compare this with the Moon, which is over 238,000 miles (380,800 km) from Earth's center. The closer a satellite is to a planet, the faster that satellite moves. It takes the Moon almost four weeks to go around the Earth. Phobos travels around Mars in 7.65 **hours**! It travels about Mars faster than Mars turns on its axis! Phobos overtakes Mars, so if you were standing on Mars' surface, you would see Phobos rise in the west, hurry across the sky, and set in the east.*

One design of a possible Mars mission vehicle. Note the streamlined shape. This would help the probe maneuver in Mars' atmosphere to slow it down during its approach. © Kurt Burmann 1986

Parachutes would allow this probe to
float gently to the surface of Mars.

An artist imagines a joint US/Soviet mission with two rovers
scurrying across the dusty surface of Mars.

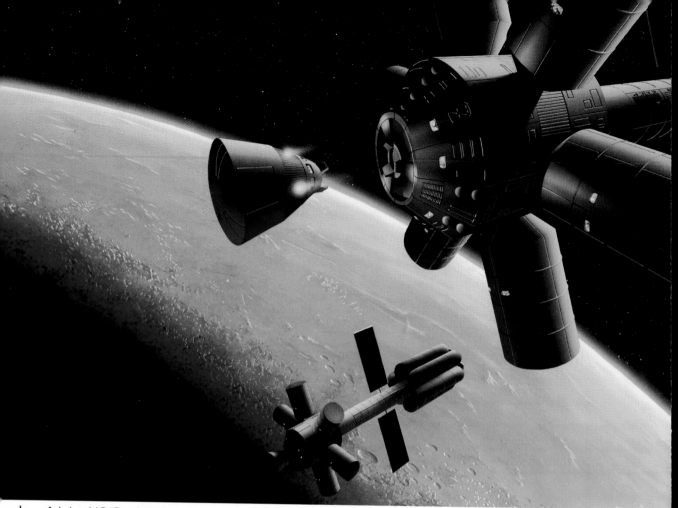

A joint US/Soviet piloted mission to Mars might be possible. The astronauts and cosmonauts could be gone from Earth for two years, so it would be helpful if the crew spoke both English and Russian!

© Doug McLeod 1987

Voyage to the Red Planet

Think of how much we'd still be wondering about Mars if not for fancy probes like Mariner and Viking. But no matter how fancy these probes might be, we could do so much more if spaceships carried astronauts to Mars. This would not be an easy task, for it might take nearly two years to go and return. Some people think it would be too big a job for any one nation.

Perhaps the United States and the Soviet Union, working together, could send a combined expedition to Mars. They could explore our mysterious neighbor, and study its craters, canyons, volcanoes, ice caps, and whatever else they find. What we learn may help us better understand our own planet, Earth.

Fog in a Martian canyon. In the background are
ice-covered mountains. Nothing is liquid on Mars
anymore, though there may once have been water
in a liquid form.

A beautiful watchtower formation at Kasei Vallis, Mars. This might
make a two-year trip to Mars worthwhile to someone who really
<u>loves</u> to travel. How about you?

21

Colonies on Mars

What else might we do if we were able to send people to Mars? We can imagine colonies on the Moon, since the Moon is only three days' rocket-time away from Earth. Mars is much farther away, but in some ways it is an easier world to live on. It has a gravitational pull that is 2/5 that of Earth, while the Moon's is only 1/6 that of Earth. Mars has a thin atmosphere that can protect people from meteors and radiation a bit, while the Moon has none. Mars has some water, while the Moon has none. We can imagine cities built underground on Mars, or perhaps domed cities on the surface. And if we do count the Moon, human beings will then be living on three different worlds.

A mission carrying people flies past Phobos and makes its final approach to the Red Planet. Crew members work on a communication satellite that will let them tell Earth's residents how they like what they find.

Mars from Phobos. To explorers stationed on Phobos,
Mars would loom large and red.

A futuristic colony on Mars. A total artificial environment — one inside
buildings, space suits, and vehicles — would make the Martian
atmosphere fit for humans. Landing at the colony would be easy
enough, and the rocket launch site would allow people to leave as well.

23

Exploring Mars

What would space explorers do on Mars? Once settlements are established on Mars, exploring parties can be sent out. Imagine some of them, in special cars, driving along the bottom of a canyon that stretches for 3,000 miles (4,800 km). Imagine a party climbing a giant volcano and studying the inside of the crater. Think of explorers making their way across the Martian ice caps at its poles. We know the ice caps contain frozen carbon dioxide, as well as frozen water. But we could learn even more about Mars from the ice caps. We might find interesting minerals, or even matter that will help us understand what Mars was like millions of years ago.

© Michael Carroll 1987

The South Pole of Mars has something major in common with Earth's South Pole — ice!

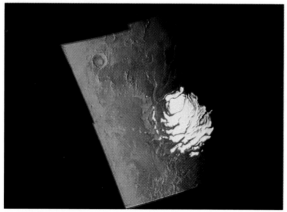

USGS

Glaciers of ice crawl across the Martian surface. Millions of years ago, creeping glaciers formed the hills and valleys of Earth with the same slow, relentless movement.

When human beings land on Mars, they can explore the insides of inactive volcanoes like this one — the Hecates Tholus Lava Tube.

The moons of Mars — a clue to life on Earth?

Phobos and Deimos don't look like Mars. Mars has a light reddish surface, but Phobos and Deimos have dark surfaces. That is probably because the satellites were once asteroids. There are certain dark meteorites that occasionally land on Earth. They contain small amounts of water and carbon-containing compounds, somewhat resembling those found in living things. Maybe it would be more interesting to study the surface of the satellites than of Mars. Wouldn't this help us decide how life originated on Earth? We'll only find out if we go there.

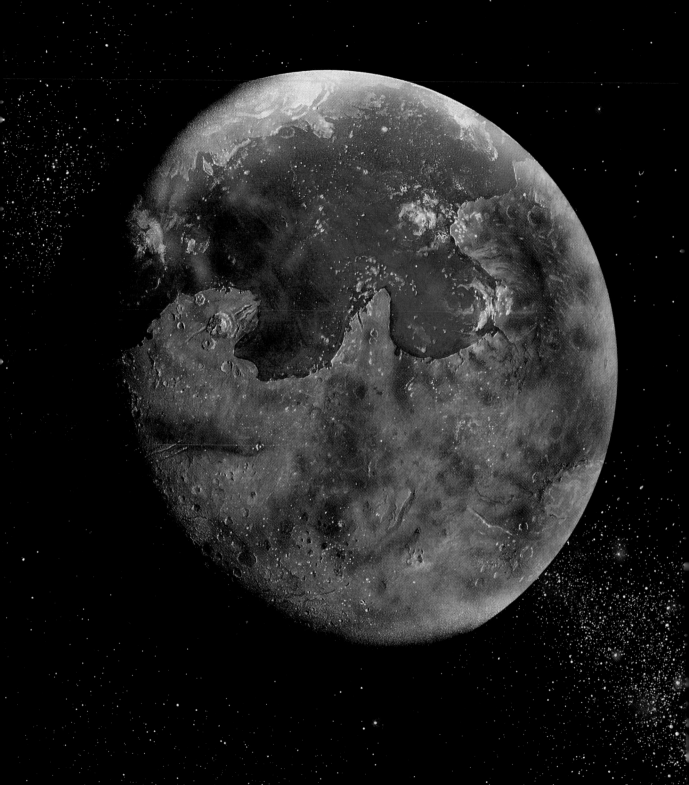

The Red and Blue Planet?

Many other, even more exciting things might be possible on Mars. The early settlers on Mars might be able to do things to make the planet more like Earth. This is called terraforming. Perhaps large supplies of water can be brought in from the asteroids. If the right gases are added to the atmosphere, Mars would trap more sunlight and grow warmer. The water won't freeze, in that case, but will form an ocean. Enough oxygen might be added to make the air breathable. Many plants and animals could be brought to Mars.

It may take many, many years, but perhaps Mars can someday become a little Earth.

On a terraformed Mars humans would not have to depend on artificial devices to breathe, keep warm or cool, or supply themselves with water. The new climate would sustain human life "naturally."

© Julian Baum 1988

Left: Here's a hot idea for the future: If we altered the climate and atmosphere of Mars by terraforming, we could melt the northern ice cap to create a large sea. © Michael Carroll 1985

Fact File: Mars

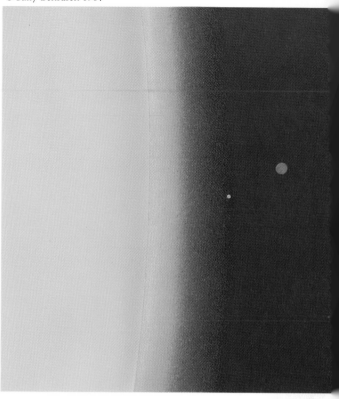

Mars is the seventh largest planet (Earth is fifth), the fourth closest to the Sun, and the first planet beyond Earth's orbit. It is also, therefore, the last of the "inner" group of planets, all of which are within the asteroid belt. Beyond the asteroids is the "outer" group that begins with Jupiter. With an axial tilt similar to Earth's and a day that is virtually the same length as ours, Mars has the same type of seasons as Earth. Of course, Mars is much farther from the Sun than Earth is, so Mars has a longer "year" than we do. This means its seasons are much longer, and its temperatures much colder, than Earth's.

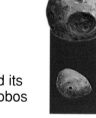

Right: Here is a close-up of Mars and its two tiny but well-known satellites, Phobos (top) and Deimos (bottom).

The Moons of Mars		
Name	Diameter	Distance From Mars' Center
Phobos	13-18 miles (20-28 km)	5,827 miles (9,378 km)
Deimos	6-10 miles (10-16 km)	14,577 miles (23,459 km)

Planet	Diameter
Mars	3,973 miles (6,786 km)
Earth	7,927 miles (12,756 km)

The Sun and Its Family of Planets

The Sun and its Solar system family, left to right, above: Mercury, Venus, Earth, Mars, Jupiter, Saturn, Uranus, Neptune, Pluto.

Mars: How It Measures Up to Earth

Rotation Period (length of day)	Period of Orbit Around Sun (length of year)	Moons	Surface Gravity	Distance from Sun (nearest-farthest)	Least Time It Takes for Light to Travel to Earth
24 hours, 37 minutes	687 days (1.88 years)	2	0.38*	129-156 million miles (207-249 million km)	3.1 minutes
23 hours, 56 minutes	365.25 days (one year)	1	1.00*	92-95 million miles (147-152 million km)	—

* Multiply your weight by this number to find out how much you would weigh on this planet.

More Books About Mars

Here are more books that contain information about Mars. If you are interested in them, check your library or bookstore.

Maria Looney on the Red Planet. Beatty (Avon)
Mars and the Inner Planets. Vogt (Franklin Watts)
Miss Pickerell Goes to Mars. MacGregor (Archway)
Our Solar System. Asimov (Gareth Stevens)
Planets. Barrett (Franklin Watts)
Rockets, Probes, and Satellites. Asimov (Gareth Stevens)

Places to Visit

You can explore Mars and other parts of the Universe without leaving Earth. Here are some museums and centers where you can find many different kinds of space exhibits.

NASA Lewis Research Center
Cleveland, Ohio

NASA Goddard Space Flight Center
Greenbelt, Maryland

Henry Crown Science Center
Museum of Science and Industry
Chicago, Illinois

Astrocentre
Royal Ontario Museum
Toronto, Ontario

For More Information About Mars

Here are some people you can write away to for more information about Mars. Be sure to tell them exactly what you want to know about. And include your full name and address so they can write back to you.

For information about Mars:
National Space Society
600 Maryland Avenue, SW
Washington, DC 20024

About missions to Mars:
NASA Kennedy Space Center
Educational Services Office
Kennedy Space Center, Florida 32899

The Planetary Society
65 North Catalina
Pasadena, California 91106

NASA Jet Propulsion Laboratory
Public Affairs 180-201
4800 Oak Grove Drive
Pasadena, California 91109

STARDATE
MacDonald Observatory
Austin, Texas 78712

Glossary

asteroids: very small planets made of rock or metal. There are thousands of them in our Solar system, and they mainly orbit the Sun between Mars and Jupiter. Some show up elsewhere in the Solar system, however, and many scientists feel that the two moons of Mars are actually "captured" asteroids.

atmosphere: the gases that surround a planet.

axis: the imaginary line through the center of a planet around which the planet rotates. The axis of Mars is tipped so that its seasons change as the planet orbits the Sun.

canal: a river or waterway made by people to move water from one place to another. It was once thought that the narrow dark markings on Mars were canals built by Martians to move water from the ice caps to the desert areas.

carbon dioxide: a heavy colorless gas that makes up 95 percent of the Martian atmosphere. When humans and other animals breathe, they exhale carbon dioxide.

colonies: human settlements. Many people have wondered if it might be possible to one day set up colonies on Mars.

craters: holes on planets and moons created by explosions or the impact of meteorites. Mars has many craters.

desert: waterless areas on land. Mars is often considered a desert planet.

extinct: no longer living, or no longer active. Both the dinosaurs and inactive volcanoes are said to be extinct.

ice cap: a cover of permanent ice at either or both ends of a planet. Mars has ice caps at both ends.

Mariner 4: a space probe that in 1965 passed within 6,000 miles (9,600 km) of Mars and photographed the planet.

Mariner 9: a probe that reached Mars in 1971, orbited the planet, and took many photographs.

Mars: the god of war in ancient Roman mythology. The planet Mars is named for him.

mass: a quantity, or amount, of matter.

Olympus Mons: a huge extinct volcano on Mars.

planet: one of the bodies that revolve around our Sun. Our Earth is one of the planets, and so is Mars.

satellite: a smaller body orbiting a larger body. Phobos and Deimos are Mars' <u>natural</u> satellites, or moons. Sputnik 1 and 2 were Earth's first <u>artificial</u> satellites.

terraforming: a way of making a planet suitable for human life.

Valles Marineris: an enormous canyon on Mars.

Viking 1 and 2: probes that actually landed on Mars and sent back information about the planet.

Index

The publishers wish to thank the following for permission to reproduce copyright material: front cover, p. 20, © Doug McLeod 1987; pp. 4, 5 (upper), 24 (left), United States Geological Survey; pp. 5 (lower), 14-15 (upper), National Space Science Data Center; p. 6, Lowell Observatory; pp. 7 (upper), 8, 10-11 (upper), 17 (upper), Jet Propulsion Laboratory; pp. 7 (lower), 9, 11 (lower), 12, 13 (upper), 14 (lower), 15 (lower), 16, courtesy of NASA; p. 10 (lower), © John Foster 1988; p. 13 (lower), © John Waite 1987; p. 26, © Michael Carroll 1985; pp. 17 (lower), 24 (right), © Michael Carroll 1987; p. 18, © Kurt Burmann 1986; p. 19 (upper), © Kurt Burmann 1987; pp. 19 (lower), 27, © Julian Baum 1988; p. 21 (upper), © David Hardy; p. 22, © Paul DiMare 1985; p. 23 (upper), © MariLynn Flynn 1985; pp. 21 (lower), 25, © MariLynn Flynn 1987; p. 23 (lower), © Ron Miller 1987; pp. 28-29, © Sally Bensusen 1987.